# HANDWRITING
## Practice for Teens

### Children's Reading & Writing Education Books

**PRODIGY**WIZARD
BOOKS

Copyright 2016

# Handwriting Exercises

Trace and rewrite the following famous quotes.

All our words from loose using have lost their edge.
 —Ernest Hemingway

All our words from loose using
have lost their edge.
 — Ernest Hemingway

There is a natural aristocracy
among men. The grounds of
this are virtue and talents.
-Thomas Jefferson

There is a natural arist
ocy among men. The grounds
of this are virtue and
talents

Without His love I can do nothing, with His love there is nothing I cannot do.

-Unknown Source

Without His love I can do nothing with His love there is nothing I cannot do.

Happiness will never come to those who fail to appreciate what they already have.

-Unknown Source

I hear and I forget, I see
and I remember. I do and I
understand.
                    -Chinese proverb

Do not confine your children
to your own learning, for they
were born in another time.
—Chinese proverb

Be not afraid of going slowly,
be afraid only of standing
still.
— Chinese proverb

God couldn't be everywhere,

so he created mothers

—Jewish proverb

omg so
true.

Love is a serious mental
disease.

-Plato

Love is as serious. mental

disease.

-Plato

Love is a serous. mental

disease.

-plato

Life can only be understood backwards, but it must be lived forward.

-Soren Kierkegaard

The one who loves least controls the relationship.

—Unknown Source

Where there is love there is
life.
                    -Mahatma Gandhi

Friendship often ends in love;
but love in friendship, never.
—Charles Caleb Colton

One day your life will flash
before your eyes. Make sure
its worth watching.
                    -Unknown Source

Life is not a problem to be
solved, but a reality to be
experienced.
                    —Soren Kierkegaard

In three words I can sum up
everything I've learned about
life. It goes on.

-Robert Frost

And in the end, it's not the
years in your life that count.
It's the life in your years.
                    -Abraham Lincoln

There is only one happiness
in life — to love and to be
loved.

-George Sand

Breakdowns can create breakthroughs. Things fall apart so things can fall together.

-Unknown Source

Teachers open the door but
you must walk through it
yourself.

 -Chinese proverb

There is no remedy for love
than to love more.
—Henry David Thoreau

A gem cannot be polished

without friction, nor a man

perfected without trials.

—Chinese proverb

Love is an act of endless
forgiveness, a tender look
which becomes a habit.
—Peter Ustinov

Follow love and it will flee,

flee love and it will follow.

—Proverb

The true sign of intelligence is
not knowledge but imagination.
—Albert Einstein

A friend walks in when everyone else walks out

-Unknown Source

The man who says his wife can't take a joke forgets that she took him.

-Unknown Source

You must be the change you
wish to see in the world.
-Mahatma Gandhi

Chose a job you love, and you
will never have to work a day
in your life.
                                    -Confucius

I have not failed. I've just found 10,000 ways that won't work.

-Thomas Alva Edison

True love is like ghosts, which everybody talks about and few have seen.

—François de La Rochefoucauld

Love is not just looking at
each other, it's looking in the
same direction.
-Antoine de Saint-Exupery

The way to love anything is
to realize that it might be
lost.
-Gilbert Keith Chesterton

Either write something worth
reading or do something
worth writing.
          -Benjamin Franklin

Happiness is when what you
think, what you say, and what
you do are in harmony.
                    -Mahatma Gandhi

Love is the beauty of the
soul.

-Saint Augustine

Made in the USA
San Bernardino, CA
20 March 2017